REVIVAL
FIRES

2015-16 NMI
MISSION EDUCATION RESOURCES

❋ ❋ ❋

BOOKS

WORLD CHANGERS
MKs and Where They Are Now
By Ellen Decker

EXTREME NAZARENE
Cross-Cultural Partners in Peru
By Pat Stockett Johnston

12:7 SERVE
Global Youth Serving in Mission
By David Gonzalez and Joel Tooley, Compilers

ONCE UPON AN ISLAND
From Farming to Fiji and Papua New Guinea
By Bessie Black

REVIVAL FIRES
The Horn of Africa Story
By Howie Shute

KINGDOM ADVANCE
in South Asia and India
By Dorli Gschwandtner and Sarah Dandge

❋ ❋ ❋

NEW ADULT MISSION EDUCATION CURRICULUM
Living Mission
Where the Church Is Not Yet

REVIVAL FIRES

The Horn of Africa Story

HOWIE SHUTE

Nazarene Publishing House
Kansas City, Missouri

Copyright © 2015 by Nazarene Publishing House
Nazarene Publishing House
PO Box 419527
Kansas City, MO 64141
www.BeaconHillBooks.com

ISBN 978-0-8341-3478-2

Printed in the
United States of America

Cover design: Jeff Gifford
Interior design: Sharon Page

The Internet addresses, email addresses, and phone numbers
in this book are accurate at the time of publication. They are
provided as a resource. Nazarene Publishing House does not en-
dorse them or vouch for their content or permanence.

10 9 8 7 6 5 4 3 2 1

Contents

1
God on the Move

*And the Lord added to their number daily
those who were being saved* (Acts 2:47).

You haven't seen anything until you've seen someone who was an avowed witch doctor place his witchcraft tools on a ceramic tile and light fire to them—and then march up and down the aisles of a formal, western-style district assembly service holding those huge, flaming tiles aloft.

Was he trying to cast some sort of spell upon our meeting and ministry?

No. This witch doctor was testifying to the fact that he had asked Jesus into his heart. And he was burning his paraphernalia for all to see, for he didn't need magic anymore. He only needed Jesus.

And actually, he was not alone. This tended to be the procedure for all witch doctors who had come to Christ and joined the Church of the Nazarene. Depending on the year and the district, we saw up to thirty men follow this practice. They were no longer walking in darkness; they were walking in the light and following Jesus Christ. And the flames shooting in the air was certainly an unforgettable way to illustrate the change in their hearts, lives, and even livelihoods.

My wife, Bev, and I had no idea what kinds of experiences were ahead of us as we joined the mass of humanity pushing toward the burdened airport conveyer belt in Addis Ababa on Christmas day in 1997. People grabbed every bag that appeared familiar, examining the tags to see if it was their own. Long lines of overloaded carts rolled to the customs officers, who searched suitcases for contraband or taxable items. An excited babble permeated the arrival hall at the Bole International Airport. Even in the airport absolutely nothing was familiar to us. We were in a completely different world.

Addis is the capital city of Ethiopia, and this city of four million people would be our new home. Our assignment was to lead the mission work for the Church of the Nazarene in Ethiopia, South Sudan, and four creative access countries.[1]

Our denomination's work in the Horn of Africa was new; only about two hundred people worshipped in our churches there. Eleven years later, those two hundred people had multiplied into approximately two hundred thousand,[2] and most of that growth occurred during our last four years in the Horn of Africa. Thousands of people came to Christ each year, along with hundreds of new churches starting. We could only describe this as a movement of God.

We witnessed some incredible transformations in people's lives—the marching witch doctors were only a small portion of the wonders we experienced.

I still remember the last time I was in one district, watching dramatized testimonies of these men who once practiced magic but now lived for Jesus. As they marched the aisles, bearing their burning testimonials, a man on the platform told his story.

This man was not a former witch doctor. He was the leader of another religion located in one of the villages in this district. He told how he had met a Nazarene who told him the truth about Jesus. He said it took a while for him to decide to leave his religion, but eventually he realized that Jesus was more than a spiritual leader, as he'd been raised to believe. He now believed with all of his heart that Jesus was the Son of God and had died to take away his sins.

"I am now a Christian," he enthusiastically proclaimed.

But that was not the end of the story. Not only had he come to Christ, but every man, woman, and child in his former place of worship had become Christians. While he finished his testimony, this former non-Christian spiritual leader handed me a set of keys and announced: "Today we are turning our place of worship over to the Church of the Nazarene."

What an incredible moment!

This kind of thing just doesn't happen, unless, of course, God is involved. And He was on the move. In fact, five buildings that were formerly used for worshipping false gods in this district have become Nazarene churches.

It really was a God-directed phenomenon. Thousands of people were coming to Christ each year, many coming out of witchcraft, large numbers leaving other religions, and multitudes abandoning other highly gospel-resistant people groups. Lives were being changed. Miracles were commonplace and communities were being transformed.

I felt as if I were living during the days we read about in the Book of Acts.

A movement of God began at Pentecost about two thousand years ago. Peter preached in the streets that day to a crowd of people who had come to Jerusalem from all over the world to worship the God of Israel.

"Those who accepted his message were baptized, and about three thousand were added to their number that day" (Acts 2:41).

From that moment the church experienced continuous expansion, first within the borders of Israel and then beyond its boundaries. Even in a casual reading of the Book of Acts we find numerous references to this continuous, explosive growth in the Church:

- "And the Lord added to their number daily those who were being saved" (Acts 2:47).
- "Many who heard the message believed, and the number of men who believed grew to about five thousand" (Acts 4:4).
- "More and more men and women believed in the Lord and were added to their number" (Acts 5:14).
- "The numbers of disciples in Jerusalem increased rapidly, and a large number of priests became obedient to the faith" (Acts 6:7).
- "The church . . . was strengthened . . . living in the fear of the Lord and encouraged by the Holy Spirit, it increased in numbers" (Acts 9:31).
- "The Lord's hand was with them, and a great number of people believed and turned to the Lord" (Acts 11:21).
- "The word of the Lord spread through the whole region" (Acts 13:49).
- "They preached the good news in that city and won a large number of disciples" (Acts 14:21).

- "The churches were strengthened in the faith and grew daily in numbers" (Acts 16:5).
- "In this way the word of the Lord spread widely and grew in power" (Acts 19:20).

The early church experienced explosive growth because God moved among His people. The Holy Spirit worked through those early believers.

The phenomenon that happened in those early years of the Church also occurred in the Horn of Africa. And this is taking place in many world areas today.

Jesus is still working through His disciples. The movement in the Book of Acts is God's standard. It is what He still wants to do throughout our world.

God's miraculous working can occur wherever the Church fulfills God's mission in His way.

God is passionate about seeing a Book of Acts movement happen in our nation and communities. However, we must implement biblical principles expressed in the Book of Acts if we will see God work today in our lives.

Many have asked me: *What was behind the movement in the Horn of Africa?*

Let's look at biblical principles that came to life behind the transformation.

2
Living in the Trenches

Five times I received from the Jews the forty lashes minus one. Three times I was beaten with rods, once I was pelted with stones, three times I was shipwrecked, I spent a night and a day in the open sea, I have been constantly on the move (2 Corinthians 11:24-26).

The Baro River was peaceful as we floated on a small boat we'd named *Good News*. We'd purchased the boat to reach villages along the border of South Sudan and Ethiopia that were so removed we could only reach them on foot or by traveling the river. The boat was aptly named since its purpose was to take the *good news of Jesus* to people living in a region of the world that would easily qualify for being *the uttermost parts of the earth*.

Though the river was peaceful, my mind was not. Other mission organizations had warned us that it was not safe to travel this river. Civil war in the

Sudan was spilling over into the Gambella Region of Ethiopia. Sudanese rebel groups resupplied their militia in this area. Tribal warfare flourished up and down the river. Malaria filled the land and a cholera epidemic was killing Sudanese villagers. And at every bend in the river crocodiles waited for unsuspecting prey.

Despite the warnings that we should not make this trip, here we were on a tranquil river heading into unknown strife.

Even though I knew God had ordained this trip, I questioned my judgment in having Bev accompany me. My wife often traveled with me but never into such a dangerous place as this.

Lord, did I do the right thing? Should Bev have come?

As I quietly communed with the Lord I saw something I had never seen before and have not seen since: a rainbow completely circled the sun. No clouds in the sky, not a trace of rain—just the colorful answer to my prayer. Without a doubt I knew God was assuring me that He would be with us on this journey.

Many centuries earlier Jesus had promised His followers that He would always be with them when they were pursuing His mission to make disciples (Matthew 28:19-20). But here was a fresh new promise. My mind rested. I was certain God would protect us and bless our efforts to take Jesus to the people living in Ethiopia and South Sudan.

Four others accompanied Bev and me. Steve, a young volunteer missionary assigned to Ethiopia, headed our JESUS Film ministry. Getamesay, our Ethiopian leader, worked with Steve to show the JESUS Film and to train church leaders to follow up on new converts.

Steve and Getamesay would show this film each night as we traveled into unreached territories. Joseph, our leader for our Sudanese mission, and Banak, our translator, were from the Nuer tribe of Sudan. It was their people group that we were coming to meet and to share God's Word with, through teaching, preaching, and the JESUS Film.

We moved downriver toward our goal of Akobo, where a growing church in that village would be organized after membership training. As the district superintendent of the Gambella District I was responsible to prepare and organize this church for membership.

Looking at the bright blue sky, Joseph mentioned that it would take twice as long to return from Akobo as it would to go there.

"What?" I asked, alarmed. I had calculated the amount of fuel we needed for the boat based on the number of days Joseph had told me it would take to reach Akobo.[1]

I had not considered that our return trip would be upriver, against a fast current. That meant we had roughly half the amount of fuel we needed to make the journey home. And that was a huge problem because there were no gas stations or places where we could purchase more fuel for our journey back to civilization.

I brought this problem to the attention of our team.

"Do you think we should proceed?" I asked.

After praying together, we all felt God wanted us to continue.

Each night Joseph selected a location where we could safely spend the night. We showed the JESUS Film there and the following morning we trained local leaders how to follow up with those who had responded to the message of this film.

We could not have any of the villagers' food or water because we would be in danger of getting cholera. We carried all of our food and water on our boat. When we cooked in the boat, we made sure flames from our little Bunsen burner did not encounter fumes from our gas cans. We frequently ate spaghetti—boil the noodles, warm prepared tomato sauce, and we were in business.

By the time we reached Burbiey we were ready for a change in menu. The villagers were so glad to see us that they killed a goat. We couldn't imagine that this goat carried the cholera disease, so we enthusiastically enjoyed this wonderful meal.

After feasting on that goat delicacy, Steve and Getamesay went into the village to set up equipment for the JESUS Film showing. Meanwhile, Bev and I welcomed to our campsite some young children who had come to teach us more of the Nuer language. Rebecca, a delightful twelve-year-old, led this small group. We enjoyed getting to know these children and learning more of their culture.

By the time the film began that evening, the entire village was present and people had also come across the river from Sudan. When the film ended, Steve and Getamesay challenged people to give their hearts and lives to Jesus. Many did.

The next morning, while our JESUS Film team taught leaders how to train new converts, I taught a church membership class to the Nazarene church in Burbiey.

As I taught the small group of people in a mud-walled, grass-roofed hut, I wondered about our safety. Men walked the village perimeter armed with AK-47s. Our makeshift classroom was filled with boxes of ammunition and with AK-47s leaning against the walls and dangling from the roof where they had been strapped.

The security measures were designed to discourage tribal enemies from coming into the village, stealing cows, and threatening the villagers. The entire wealth of the people in this village was measured in how many cows they owned.

But in this hut, so different from what I knew, a number of people agreed to accept the doctrine of the church and live according to its standards. A church was organized.

All of this took place as others were being trained to disciple new Christians. The discipleship class only experienced one distraction: a king cobra raised its regal hood and peered into their outdoor classroom, but the students barely noticed the intruder.

We rose early the next morning to continue our journey down the Gilo and on to Akobo. We were getting ready to load our boat when a village man approached us. He said a child had gotten cholera and appeared lifeless. He explained that a while earlier a medical team had stopped in their village to give them IV packs to use for anyone who got cholera. But no one knew how to use these IV packs, and he implored us to help this child.

"But I have no training! I've never put an IV into someone's arm," I explained.

He turned to Bev, but she also refused. He went to Steve and others in our team. He kept repeating, "She will die if you do not help her!"

"Look, I don't know how to use an IV pack, but I do know how to pray," I finally said. I went to the village to see this girl. When I entered the home, she was lying on the floor.

I gasped. It was Rebecca, that precious girl who had taught us some of her language. Her mother and father wept, sure that they had lost their daughter.

I asked Jesus to fill her body with the fluids she needed to bring her through this disease. I asked Jesus for a complete healing. I hated leaving the family with their grief, but I could only leave them in the hands of a merciful and loving God.

On our boat again, we left the Baro River, taking the Gilo south to where we would pick up the Akobo River, heading west to the village of Akobo. On our way to Akobo we planned to stop and organize a new church in another village along the Gilo.

As we approached the village we knew something was wrong. The village was gone!

We later learned that the villagers had fled from armed cattle rustlers. Again I was amazed at how people lived in this part of the world.

Later that day we picked up the Akobo River and started on the last stretch of river to Akobo. The sun was high overhead when we approached Wang-ding, Sudan. We had not planned to stop in this village, but we encountered a barrier of undergrowth that choked all river traffic. Our boat would not pass through this heavy vegetation, even as we charged it at full throttle.

And the vegetation continued like that as far as we could see.

Now what? The church in Akobo expected us, but we would never reach them by boat. We asked for the Lord's guidance and believed we should continue. But our only alternative was to walk—thirty miles overland, which would take ten hours.

We left Getamesay in Wangding since we couldn't carry all of the JESUS Film equipment along with our sleeping bags, tents, and food. So Getamesay stayed to guard the boat and to carry on the JESUS Film ministry until we returned.

Since we carried heavy loads, enduring the high temperatures was more difficult than before. Joseph and Banak offered to carry our loads. We were tempted to relinquish our burdens to them, but figured we only had to walk three hours before we needed to find a secure area to sleep.

We arose before the sun the next day and continued the journey westward. After walking for several hours, we sat on a log to rest near a few homes.

Joseph began talking with people from this tiny settlement. When we were ready to continue the journey he told us he'd catch up with us, which he did an hour later.

Again, the temperatures were high and our loads heavy. Then the rain began. At first Bev was excited about a shower to cool our bodies—until we were completely soaked and the winds picked up. We went from being overheated to chilled.

To make matters worse the dusty trails turned to adhesive mud. Our shoes became elevators, raising us several inches above the ground. As we walked Joseph used a stick to try to strike mud from the bottoms of Bev's shoes.

By now Bev and I no longer resisted our leaders' insistence to carry our packs. We gladly turned them over to these gracious men.

When we straggled into Akobo our bodies shook uncontrollably from the falling temperatures. We were covered with mud, and we were exhausted. As we trudged into the village our church people welcomed us with song. Then the ladies of the church removed our shoes. This is the tradition of Sudanese Nuer Christians—they routinely wash their guests' feet.

I had experienced this many times before, but this day more than our feet got washed. They washed our bodies from head to toe. They took our shoes to the river and thoroughly cleaned them.

The reception was amazing. We went to the pastor's grass-roofed hut and he brought dry clothes for us to put on. He could not find anything for Bev, so he brought her a mosquito net. She found that if she wrapped it around herself many times, the netting became opaque.

We were starved. When we left the boat, we had also left behind most of our supplies. We had packed one small can of beans or Vienna sausage per person per day, but that did not supply the energy our bodies required. We could not eat the village food because of the fear of cholera. The pastor brought us a large jar of honey, which we thought would be free from cholera-producing bacteria. So Steve, Bev, and I shared the jar of sweet nectar.

"Now I understood why the Bible tells us that Jonathan's eyes were shining after he took honey from the comb," Bev said. The honey was a bountiful feast.

After rest and nourishment we visited the village elders. As guests in this village we needed to seek permission to stay there and to let them know about our ministry plans for their village.

When we walked into their council room they greeted us enthusiastically. We told them what we were doing in their region and that we had come to share Jesus and train church members in their village. They told us that we were the first white people who had ever reached their village. They appreciated our intent and thanked us for coming.

As we talked I noticed five jerry cans in the corner of their meeting room and asked what was in them. I was glad to hear they were filled with gasoline.

"Would you sell us three of those cans?" I asked.

"No, no. Without our gas our boat cannot reach Gambella. We have nowhere to buy gas," they explained. They had purchased this fuel from Sudanese rebels who had passed through their village. They had no idea when another opportunity would arise, so they were determined to hold onto their fuel.

We talked more about our ministry and then asked again about buying fuel. According to my calculations, we needed three cans to return to Gambella, but maybe the Lord would stretch two of them to get us back home.

Finally the elders agreed to give us two cans, but they refused to take money.

"You are serving our people, so we will give you two cans," they said. They promised to deliver the cans to our tents later.

Back at our tents, we saw three ladies with jerry cans perched upon their heads. The Lord provided three cans of fuel, the full amount we needed to make our journey back to Gambella.

We taught most of that next day. Nearly three hundred people stood before the altar vowing membership as I organized this, our remotest church in Ethiopia. What a great time we had teaching and preaching and worshipping Jesus together.

At four the next morning we began our journey back to Wangding, Sudan, where Getamesay and our boat waited. We now had our gear to carry back to the boat, along with three five-gallon cans of fuel. That was not a problem, however: Three ladies appeared, lifted these heavy gasoline cans to their heads, and took off ahead of us at breakneck speed.

The temperature got hot later that day, but we were thrilled to be on our way to our supplies. Our stomachs were empty and we ran out of drinking water. Fortunately we had water filters, so we braved the muddy, cholera-laden river water. We had to filter and then refilter before the cloudy brown water looked anything like drinking water. We hoped the extra filtration took care of the cholera threat. There was no choice—we had to have water, or we would not reach the boat.

As we walked through the settlement where we had rested on our way to Akobo, we saw that a new church facility was under construction. Men were thatching the roof with grass. Joseph told us the people he had talked to were building a worship facility, our newest church plant in this region of Ethiopia.

We were still a good distance from Wangding when the three ladies who had taken our fuel passed us, having delivered our fuel to the boat already. These were some of the most rugged people I had ever met, yet they treated their guests so hospitably.

When we arrived in Wangding Getamesay had dinner waiting for us. It was spaghetti again—and it had never tasted better. He also hard-boiled some eggs. We feasted with thanksgiving. Getamesay had shown the JESUS Film each night, and many people in the village had begun a walk with Jesus.

After spending the night in that village, we got into our boat to go home. We had been gone for two weeks, and still had a few more days before we would reach our vehicle in Gambella. Then we would drive two days before we would be back in our own beds.

Eventually we reached that junction of the Gilo and Baro rivers, just outside of the village of Burbiey. We pulled to shore just before reaching the Baro and asked people along the river's edge, "How's Rebecca?"

We almost jumped out of the boat when we heard that she had completely recovered from that terrible disease. In these remote villages people die from cholera and other diseases almost daily unless God intervenes. And that is exactly what He did.

We had seen so many people dying on this trip because of the lack of proper medical attention. Cholera and malaria were killing them, and they had to depend upon God just to make it through the day.

Life is hard on the river. Sharing the Good News with these people was like throwing lifelines to drowning people.

As we pushed away from the river's edge, we approached the Baro River, where we would turn eastward toward home. Near that junction, Banak looked under seats and searched every corner of the boat.

"Howie, we have a problem," Banak exclaimed. "The tennis shoes are missing!"

"What shoes?"

When we had showed the JESUS Film in Burbiey a week earlier, a young man had come across the river by boat to see this film. After the film he had stayed to ask questions about Jesus and had missed his ride home. That meant he had to swim back, but he did not want to get his new tennis shoes wet and left the shoes with Banak for safekeeping.

Since the man had not returned before our departure from Burbiey, Banak had put the man's shoes under the seat at the bow of the boat, expecting to return them on our way back through this village.

But someone had stolen the tennis shoes from the boat in Wangding.

"Don't worry, Banak," I said. "Tell the man we'll buy him a new pair and send them to him after we get back to Addis Ababa."

"You don't understand," Banak told me, fretting.

We turned eastward onto the Baro and saw a group of young men standing on the Sudanese side of the river. One was the man looking for his tennis shoes.

Banak yelled across the river, informing the man that his shoes had been stolen and that we would replace them.

This man was not impressed. He was not holding a rifle, but others carried AK-47s. He quickly grabbed an assault rifle from his friend's hands and turned the weapon on us. Before he could squeeze the trigger, his companions jumped on him and took away the weapon.

He grabbed a weapon from another man. Again, his friends wrestled the weapon away from him. This occurred several times.

"Hurry, Steve! Faster!" I begged.

"I'm driving as fast as I can!" Steve exclaimed, his eyes huge and terrified. Unfortunately, we were going against the fast-moving current—which limited our speed to about three miles per hour.

So while this man was trying to kill us, we slowly maneuvered up the river. Finally we were out of sight of our would-be murderer and were elated that the Lord had protected us.

"It's almost sunset. We need to find a safe place for the night," Joseph announced.

"But we can't stop yet," I countered. "That guy is still mad about his shoes. If we stop, he'll catch up with us. We don't want him to find us sleeping in our tents and kill us."

"But we must stop," Joseph insisted. "It is *impossible* to safely navigate the waters at night."

My fear of what lay behind us was greater than my fear of what lay ahead, so we continued.

Piiing! At 2 a.m. the first shot whistled above us.

We saw the crowd of men who had sent a warning shot from the Sudan side.

"Bring your boat . . . come to shore *now!*" they demanded.

"No! You are thieves," Joseph yelled. "We will not come to shore."

The next bullet was even closer than before, and we knew we had no choice. We turned the boat toward the shore and hoped for the best.

Bev had been sleeping under a tarp. I warned her to stay out of sight. I had no idea what would happen if these armed men found out we had a woman aboard.

We quickly realized that a Sudanese rebel militia was accosting us. They took Joseph to a nearby hut and questioned him.

Next it was my turn. The commander of this rebel army came to the boat and asked, "Who are you? What are you doing here?"

As the questions continued I realized they were comparing Joseph's answers and mine. Eventually the commander said, "You are serving God and our people. You may go."

As we pulled away from shore, Joseph said, "This is very unusual. Usually in these cases they would kill us and take our boat and all of our supplies."

"After this miracle I expect to see Jesus tonight walking on the water," Getamesay added.

Steve steered us safely down those dark waters the rest of the night. Getamesay kept watch while the rest of us slept. An hour or two later I heard Getamesay laughing.

I peered out from under the tarp and saw Getamesay almost dancing, exclaiming, "I told you we would see Jesus tonight."

It was an incredible sight. I cannot tell you how many fish were in the air all at one time. It was a feeding frenzy with large Nile perch flying through the air. I had never seen anything like it. Getamesay was convinced that Jesus was showing us His hand.

I still remember the bridge that stretched across the river as we approached Gambella. I had always thought of Gambella as a long way from nowhere, but that morning I felt as if we were approaching New York City. After all, Gambella had stores where we could resupply, restaurants where we could purchase nice meals, and hotels with comfortable beds.

Before we docked, I checked our gasoline supply. God had supplied the gasoline in a place where none was usually available and we even had half a can left.

I remembered that unusual rainbow circling the sun as we headed for Akobo. That rainbow had been God's message to me that He would protect us and bless us.

He had given that promise long before we saw the rainbow. He promised His disciples that if they would go into His world and make disciples, He would be with them even to the end of the age.

The whole journey from Addis Ababa to Gambella to Akobo and back took three unforgettable weeks. And fifty new churches were planted along the river in South Sudan and Ethiopia because of that trip and later follow-up.

I have always believed ministry takes place in the trenches. Although computers, email, web sites, and office support are helpful in ministry, they can also distract us. Christian leaders need to be in the trenches where the people are. Leaders need to take Jesus to the people and not wait for people to come to them. Christians need to take risks and enter the difficult situations people face.

The Apostle Paul lived in the trenches. He stood in opposition to the religious establishment of the day and was flogged five times as a result. He was also stoned and beaten with rods. He traveled long distances to reach the lost. Three times he was shipwrecked. He spent extended time on the seas. He was constantly on the move.

Paul presents a model for ministry that moves us out of our comfort zones and into the trenches where the spiritual battles of ministry are won.

Our people in the Horn lived in the trenches. They did not cloister themselves behind the church walls. They moved to wherever they found the lost.

In the trenches the rubber meets the road in ministry.

Living in the trenches was one of the biblical principles behind the movement in the Horn of Africa.

3
The Man of God

After they prayed, the place where they were meeting was shaken (Acts 4:31).

Pray for us that the message of the Lord may spread rapidly (2 Thessalonians 3:1).

I looked for someone among them who would build up the wall and stand before me in the gap on behalf of the land (Ezekiel 22:30).

Ethiopians who know Zekarias have given him the name Man of God in respect for the way he lives. He lives in Chano Mille, a small village in Southern Ethiopia, and provides for his family by growing and selling fruit. He's an old man with a third grade education and is a pastor in the Church of the Nazarene.

Pastor Zekarias has a heart for God and people. That heart drove him to act a number of years ago when communism brought atheism to his country. People were being taught that God did not exist. One day Zekarias took Bibles to a communist administrative compound in his area. This was simply a walled-in area with several buildings housing administrative offices where many atheists worked. As he entered the compound gate, a guard stopped him.

"What is in your box?" he demanded to know.

"I am bringing Bibles to give to people who work here," Zekarias replied.

"You will not bring those Bibles in here!" the guard shouted. "In fact, you will throw them into the fire!"

He pointed to an intensely burning baker's oven just inside the gate.

Zekarias blurted out, "This is the Word of God. I would never destroy the Word of God."

"If you do not throw the Bibles in that fire, I will make you put your arm in the fire!" the guard warned.

"I'd rather burn my arm than to destroy even one of these Bibles," Pastor Zekarias answered.

The guard dragged Zekarias to the fire and forced him to put his arm into the flames rising from the hot coals. But when Pastor Zekarias removed his arm the skin showed no burns.

The guard stared in surprise. Then he commanded, "Put your arm in again and this time leave it until I tell you to take it out."

Pastor Zekarias put it in again. Again, the arm was unburned and uninjured.

Just then a superior officer came through the gate and saw the Bibles.

"Soldier, what are these Bibles doing here? Throw them into the fire!"

"No, sir, not me, not after what I just saw," the guard responded.

This story from the days when communists ruled Ethiopia illustrates Pastor Zekarias's heart. He would do anything for his God and for those who do not know Jesus.

Pastor Zekarias is also a man of prayer. Many nights when people are sleeping, he walks through their villages and lays his hands on houses, praying for those living there. He prays that God will enter those homes and penetrate the people's hearts, tearing down the barriers keeping them from Jesus. And then in days to come he returns to those homes and tells the inhabitants about the gospel.

Chano Mille is near two beautiful lakes, surrounded by mountain peaks. Pastor Zekarias has claimed one of those peaks as his prayer mountain. Many nights Zekarias will climb to the top of that mountain and lie facedown with his arms extended over his head. He then prays for everyone living in the direction his arms are pointing. During the night he rotates his body like the hands of a clock, always praying for people in the direction where his arms point. He prays until he has made a complete circle.

When he prays to the south, he is praying for the people of southern Ethiopia and Kenya. Praying to the west, he is asking God to move among those southwestern tribes of Ethiopia and into Sudan; to the north the northern Ethiopians and those in Eritrea and Djibouti; and to the east he prays for the Sidama and other eastern tribes of Ethiopia and into Somalia.

Night after night, year after year, Pastor Zekarias has prayed for God to move in the Horn of Africa.

Pastor Zekarias contacted me one day with an important message.

"Pastor Howie, last night I spent my night on my prayer mountain. Just before morning I saw something I have never seen. Fire fell all around my mountain. In every direction. Get ready! God is about to move in the Horn of Africa. The Holy Spirit will do some amazing things."

Looking back, I can see that God started to move the year Pastor Zekarias shared that vision with me. Until that time the Church of the Nazarene was planting about 50 churches a year in the Horn of Africa.

But the year Pastor Zekarias told me about his vision we planted 283 new churches. The next year

Nazarenes planted nearly 600 churches, and the year after that approximately 1,000 new churches were planted in the Horn of Africa.

God's people have to live and minister in the trenches. That's where people are reached. That's where God works. And yet our striving will not bring about a revival unless everything is bathed in prayer.

Behind the growth in the Horn of Africa was concerted, passionate prayer by Zekarias and others. Zekarias held onto God year after year, believing God would bring multitudes into His kingdom. Nazarenes in the Horn believe in prayer, and they still seek God and His transformation upon their people.

The early church members in the Book of Acts were devoted to prayer and believed that God moved when they prayed. The prophet Ezekiel said that God looked for a person who would stand in the gap on behalf of his or her nation.

Behind every movement you will find people who have given their lives and cried out to God to heal their land. It was so in the Book of Acts. It was so in the Horn of Africa. It is true wherever God is working.

4

Power Evangelism

Now, Lord, consider their threats and enable your servants to speak your word with great boldness. Stretch out your hand to heal and perform miraculous signs and wonders through the name of your holy servant Jesus (Acts 4:29-30).

When the crowds heard Philip and saw the miraculous signs he performed, they all paid close attention to what he said (Acts 8:6).

Sana[1] listened to her doctor's solemn prognosis. She was a Muslim. Her doctor was a Muslim. Seventy percent of the town was Muslim.

"I have no hope for you. The medicine I have given you for the HIV/AIDS virus is no longer helping. My advice is to find someone to help you to your home, find a place to lie down, and there you will die."

Sana was heartbroken; she was not ready to die.

Some people helped Sana get home. They placed her on a mattress on the floor. And they left. No one would return to help her. They were afraid of this virus that was killing so many. They did not know how the disease spread. They felt sorry for her, but no one wanted to risk catching this terrible disease.

Sana became weaker until she could no longer get up from her mattress, even to use the bathroom. So there she lay, along with her bodily waste.

The small Nazarene church in that town was only about a year old. The pastor heard of Sana's plight. He did not know her. He only knew that she was Muslim and was dying from AIDS. He visited her.

When the pastor saw her lying in that pitiful condition, his heart broke and he wept. He knelt by her, placed his hands on her, and began to pray.

Next the pastor begged some ladies of his church to minister to this woman. These ladies gave Sana a bath, washed her clothing, cleaned her mattress, and prayed for her. One lady even fed her, hand to mouth, since Sana was too weak to drink and eat on her own.

After a while Sana regained some strength. Eventually, she could get off the mattress and take care of her own needs.

"I am going back to see my doctor!" she decided.

When she found her doctor, she said, "Doctor, when you sent me home, you told me that I had no hope, but today I have hope. For the first time in my life I am not afraid to die. Some friends told me about Jesus. He is my Lord and Savior. I now have hope."

Sana told the doctor that she wanted more of the medicine she had previously taken.

"If the medicine helps me live even a few months more, I want to take it. Then I can tell everyone that Jesus is more than a prophet. He can forgive sins and give us eternal life," she said.

"I'm not sure about this Jesus stuff, but I can run some tests and see what dosage you need," the doctor replied.

After the tests and his evaluation the doctor exclaimed: "I can't give you the medicine."

Sana's heart sunk.

"But why?" she asked.

"Because you no longer need it!" he declared. "I have never seen anyone cured of AIDS. I don't understand it!"

Sana smiled as she pointed her finger upward. "Doctor, Jesus must have touched me. Jesus has given me a miracle!"

"I don't know about Jesus, but you have had a miracle from somewhere!"

Sana told everyone in the town how Jesus had taken away her sins and given her eternal life. Everyone knew she had been dying of AIDS, so they paid close attention to her testimony because of this miracle. Many became Christians. In fact, she joined the church of the pastor who had prayed for her, and this church grew from seventy people to nearly a thousand.

God often uses miracles to increase the effectiveness of evangelism. We see this repeatedly in the Book of Acts. We see this in the revival in Samaria, where crowds paid close attention to Philip because of the miracles Jesus performed through him (Acts 8:6). We read it again when Peter and John healed the beggar at the temple gate called Beautiful and many listened to their teaching as a result (Acts 3:11).

The religious authorities arrested Peter and John because they taught people about Jesus' death and resurrection. After warning them to speak no longer about Jesus, they set them free.

Peter and John then asked God for boldness to continue speaking about Jesus in the face of this opposition. The early church understood that miracles captured the attention of those resisting the gospel message. That understanding was manifested in their prayer when they cried to God, "Stretch out your hand to heal and perform signs and wonders through the name of your holy servant Jesus" (Acts 4:30).

In the Horn of Africa ill and physically incapacitated people were healed, the deaf heard again, and demon-possessed people were set free. Even someone stricken with AIDS was cleansed of her disease.

Power evangelism (people coming to Christ through miracles) was another factor behind the movement in the Horn of Africa.

It's time for the Church to once again pray in faith: "Stretch out your hand to heal and perform signs and wonders through the name of your holy servant Jesus."

5

A Holy Mission

*But you will receive power when the Holy Spirit
comes on you; and you will be my witnesses in
Jerusalem, and in all Judea and Samaria,
and to the ends of the earth* (Acts 1:8).

In his early years Kareso had a reputation as
a fighter. That all changed the day he surrendered
to Jesus. Kareso began a new life and became a respected businessman in Bona,[1] where he and his wife
owned a restaurant.

After Kareso gave his heart to Jesus, he attended
a church in his community. At first he was enthu-
siastic about his new faith, but eventually his faith
was undermined with relentless discouragement. He
became disappointed in the church because the lives
of Christians were no different from those outside
of the church. His relationship with Jesus grew cold.

One day a Nazarene evangelist traveled through
Kareso's village, but Kareso was not impressed. He

told the evangelist he was skeptical of the church because of Christians' lives.

Our evangelist explained that Jesus died not only to take away our outward sins but also to cleanse us of the self-centered nature that caused those sins. He explained that Jesus could keep our spirits, souls, and bodies blameless before the Lord, as we experienced this cleansing.

"It is God's will that we be sanctified," the evangelist instructed, "and He calls us to live a holy life."

This bearer of Good News explained that many Christians were ignorant of this call or did not want to give their lives fully to God.

Kareso was fascinated. His heart burned in the following days as he studied scriptures about this teaching. As he became convinced of this truth, Kareso fell to his knees and offered himself completely to Jesus.

"Lord, I know You are calling me to holiness and that You are faithful and will keep Your word and sanctify me entirely."

The townspeople had noticed the changes in Kareso's life when he first began to follow Jesus, but they were amazed at these new changes. Kareso's love for people became more evident through his smiling eyes and compassionate actions.

Something significant has happened to Kareso, they thought.

Kareso could no longer remain silent about his faith. He told everyone about Jesus and His ability to transform their lives. He told them about God's calling to live a holy life, and he taught them how to enter that holy life.

People came to his house to hear more. Kareso never planned to begin a church in his home, but there were no Nazarene churches in his town. For that matter, no church of any denomination taught this truth in his vicinity, so he began holding regular meetings in his home with people searching for God.

When I met Kareso I marveled at his wide smile and sensed an unmistakable depth of love as he warmly welcomed me. He told me his church did not usually meet on Monday nights, but since I was in their town, the people wanted to hear me preach.

"Pastor Howie, preach on holiness," he said. "Our people want to know more about this wonderful truth."

Sidama people jump up and down as they sing to express the joy bubbling from their hearts. And on this night their hearts overflowed. Many townspeople had joined the church people and all would not fit in the house. As I preached, I noticed many standing outside Kareso's home. Windows were filled with interested faces, and I saw many standing in the muddy street beyond them.

As I preached about the cleansing fire that fills our lives when Jesus baptizes us with the Holy Spirit, I knew the fire set in that fledgling church would spread far beyond its four walls. However, I would have never guessed how intense and far-reaching that fire would be.

The movement of God in the Horn of Africa was a holiness transformation as men and women like Kareso searched for more of God and were passionate about the scriptural truths leading to holy lives.

Holiness propelled the Church in the Horn of Africa just as holiness had fueled the movement in the Book of Acts. Jesus had commanded His disciples to go into all the world and make disciples (Matthew 28:19-20). The urgency was clear, but something critical must take place in their lives for them to successfully fulfill this mission. Jesus instructed His disciples to wait in Jerusalem until they received the gift the Father had promised. They needed first to be baptized by the Holy Spirit (Acts 1:4-5). And this baptism would provide the power they needed be His witnesses.

One hundred and twenty disciples patiently waited. That sound like a violent wind coming from heaven was the first indication for these disciples that they were about to receive the gift the Father had promised.

As they looked at the flames resting on the heads of their fellow believers, they must have understood that this was an outward sign of an inward cleansing. God, who had revealed himself in fire when He spoke to Moses in the burning bush and when He guided the Hebrews through the desert in the night, was coming to His people again in symbolic fire. This cleansing fire of God was entering the disciples' lives, fulfilling their final preparation for the mission.

The change of heart was undeniable. These reticent and self-absorbed followers of Jesus became transformed in a moment. Before this Pentecostal experience, these disciples were focused on who was the greatest among them.[2] They disowned Jesus when their lives were in jeopardy.[3] Not so after the Holy Spirit's baptism. As soon as the Spirit came upon them, they rushed into the streets and, risking their own lives, proclaimed God's Word.[4]

This gift of God is not an option. Without this heart cleansing we live with our own interests at center. But when Pentecost comes the believer's priority becomes the glory of God and the salvation of the lost. We are compelled into the streets, into the marketplaces, into the schools, and into the places of business—wherever people are found—with the wonderful message that Jesus saves.

The message and experience of holiness is at the foundation of every movement of God. The early church recognized this. That's why they gave Spirit baptism the highest priority as they discipled new believers.[5] **Holiness was a driving force behind the movement recorded in the Book of Acts. And it was a driving force behind the movement in the Horn of Africa.** Miracles capture unbelievers' attention but not as much as Spirit-filled believers who live the message they preach.

6

Multiplying Disciples, Multiplying Churches

Make disciples of all nations, baptizing them . . .
and teaching them to obey everything I have
commanded you (Matthew 28:19-20).

The church in Kareso's home worshiped together for eight months before my first visit to Bona and had grown to 80 people. On the night I was there, 240 crowded into that small home. And what a worship service! Many gave their hearts to Jesus. Others consecrated their lives to God and were sanctified.

Kareso said he wanted to take me to see a church his church had planted. I was pleased to hear that they had already planted a church, but I told him they *should* have planted a church by now.

"That's our DNA," I pointed out. Every church in the Horn of Africa was expected to plant a church every six months, and the leaders trained and encouraged this new church to plant a church that would in return reproduce itself.[1]

"Howie, you misunderstand," Kareso replied. "We have not planted one church. We have planted five churches. We don't have time for you to see all five so we will visit this one."

The church was about an hour's drive in my four-wheel drive Toyota. As we approached the meeting place, I was amazed to see that the people had already constructed a worship facility, complete with benches and an altar. This church was only three months old and already had about 120 worshippers!

I was not surprised to find the people of this new church passionate about holiness since holiness was embedded into the DNA of Kareso's ministry.

As we left that church Kareso announced, "Now we will go to the church this church has planted."

Think of it! Kareso's eight-month-old church was a grandmother—three generations of churches started in eight months.

This granddaughter church took us more than an hour to reach, straight up over a mountain. My truck's wheels straddled a dry riverbed much of the way. Finally Kareso announced, "Turn right here!"

No path was visible, but I did see a break in the tree line. As I drove through the opening, about five hundred people moved toward us, jumping up and down and singing as they welcomed us.

Ermias, our country coordinator for Ethiopia at the time, told me this church was about one month old and the hillside was their sanctuary.

We worshipped together. At one point the children came to the front to sing. Their faces and voices overflowed with exuberance. I was so impressed with what God had done through Kareso and those working with him.

"Where did these people come from?" I asked Ermias.

"Howie, these people were tree worshippers one month ago," he said.

I saw the children continue to sing, but it was suddenly like someone turned down the volume of the worship service, and that still, small voice said, "Howie, this movement is much bigger than you."

This was the first moment I realized we were in the midst of a genuine movement of God. And when God works, people come to Jesus by the thousands and churches are planted by the hundreds. A culture of multiplication was occurring in the Church in the Horn of Africa. And it was happening one disciple at a time.

After his personal Pentecost, Kareso shared his love for Jesus throughout his community, and many people followed Jesus. He then led these new disciples into the experience of entire sanctification.[2] He mentored leaders to make disciples who made disciples and to plant churches that would plant churches.

Kareso focused first in Bona and then traveled to villages throughout his region. He gave such priority to the Great Commission that he was often away from home.

One day his wife cautioned, "Kareso, I am committed to the Great Commission, but our restaurant is failing because you are gone so much. We still have to feed our family and send our children to school," she reminded him. "That costs money and we need customers."

Kareso and his wife prayed and God directed. His wife was to run the restaurant and Kareso was to continue planting churches.

The villages around Bona depended upon this town for trade. Twice a week people of surrounding villages came to Bona for market days. And when they came, they ate lunch at Kareso's restaurant. The more churches that were planted in these villages, the greater the number of Nazarenes who would travel to Bona on market days and wait in line to have their lunch at Kareso's restaurant.

The day came when Kareso's wife told him they had a problem with the restaurant again.

"Are we still losing customers?" he asked.

"No, no, no! We have *too many* customers," she explained. "They have to wait in line outside for lunch, standing in that scorching midday sun. I tell them to go eat somewhere else since I can't feed them quickly enough. But they won't go! They say no one has ever cared for them like you have—you loved them enough to come to their village and share Jesus with them. So they will only eat in your restaurant."

The two prayed again and the Lord prompted them to start another restaurant. His wife managed the two restaurants, and Kareso continued traveling, making more disciples and planting churches.

Again long lines formed, now outside his two restaurants.

"Your best business plan is to plant more churches!" I joked with Kareso one day.

Kareso started that little house church in a region of Ethiopia that had no Nazarene churches. This layman was passionate about the lost. The church grew, one disciple at a time. These disciples made disciples until a thousand members joined the Bona church. And hundreds of churches rose across the region. Disciples were making disciples and churches were planting churches.

Kareso became the zone leader, and these multiplying churches became an organized district of 250 churches. Kareso was ordained and elected as the first district superintendent.[3] A whole district of churches was born out of a small church in Kareso's home.

Despite an ongoing struggle with diabetes, Kareso gave his life to reaching the lost. When he died after losing both kidneys, twenty thousand people came to his funeral.

Many came to Jesus through Kareso's witness, some from the witness of his family. One of his own brothers was elected as the next superintendent of this new district. Kareso's legacy had been established, and Jesus was fulfilling His promise to build His church, even in this southeastern region of Ethiopia.

Jesus promised that He would build the Church, but His plan is to accomplish this through His disciples making disciples who make disciples.

Jesus gave this mission to His disciples during His last forty days on earth with them. During those days Jesus focused on one thing: His disciples were to make disciples.

He also talked to them about being baptized with the Holy Spirit, but that experience was to prepare them for their disciple-making mission.

The movement that took place in the Book of Acts was one of multiplication—disciples multiplying disciples and churches multiplying churches. And this was an extremely important factor behind the movement in the Horn of Africa.

7
A Culture of Training

And the things that you have heard me say in the
presence of many witnesses entrust to reliable people
who will also be qualified to teach others
(2 Timothy 2:2).

Yual was born in a remote village in South Sudan. His mother had already birthed two children who had died as infants. So this child was named *Yual*, meaning, "one who will die soon before he grows up."

Yual's parents worshipped two gods whom they believed created the river, rocks, and other ordinary objects. With no church in Yual's village, he had no exposure to Christianity.

Yual also lacked education. Tribal warfare was rampant in his country. Nutritional and medical resources were scarce. And with a name like *Yual*, little hope existed for this child.

The only sign of hope was that Yual was the last-born child of his mother, and the last born in their culture received inheritance rights. Being last born and the only surviving child meant the gods had protected him. So he would be considered special and highly respected in the community. Many would listen to his counsel as this young child became a man.

When Yual was eleven years old a man in his community died, and Yual began to think about death. He became disturbed and could not stop crying. He worried constantly about the afterlife, but his religion was silent on this subject. In his culture children could not ask questions about death because this subject brought fear to the community. Yual wondered about Christianity. He knew a Protestant church was five miles from his village, but he didn't know if the church's gods had any answers for him.

When Yual was fifteen years old his uncle visited their home and told Yual about the gospel. Yual was amazed that there was only one God and this God loved him enough to die for him. Yual attended church with his uncle and became a believer. He was baptized and given the Christian name John.

The war in his country drove many, including John, into another nation, into a refugee camp. While there, John found the Church of the Nazarene.

"In the midst of much suffering and hopelessness the Church of the Nazarene shared the gospel with us," John said.

John heard the message of holiness and hungered for the heart cleansing that Jesus promised. He asked God to sanctify his heart.

This experience changed John's life. Even though his country was at war and he lived in a refugee camp, he experienced a deep sense of peace. And God gave him a burden for his people. He desperately wanted to share the message of holiness with them.

John became a pastor for the Church of the Nazarene in his refugee camp. That was when I first met him. I had arranged a week of training for new pastors in Addis Ababa. John came to this and was one of the best students in his class. I was impressed not only with his academic abilities but also with his character and his passion for ministry.

We invited John to be one of our leaders when we created a new school for our pastors, Creative Leadership Institute (CLI). The pastors would be trained while they continued their ministry in their local churches.

John became a certified teacher and traveled to Addis Ababa for two pastoral training classes every three months. Then he returned to his district and taught those classes to pastors in his area.

As the school developed, we had three levels of training. In the first level our Trainers of Teachers were taught in three different field-training centers in the Horn. After three weeks of classes (sixty hours per class), these trainers would go to our district centers and prepare our teachers in those same two classes. They would train in the main language of the districts. The courses were then condensed into two weeks of training (forty hours per class).

After the teachers completed their study, they returned to their zones to teach pastors in their mother tongues. Pastors were then challenged to teach the same curriculum to their congregants. Everyone who received training was expected to reteach what they had learned. We developed a teach-reteach culture.

Students at every level in this school had an active pastoral ministry and pursued the Church of the Nazarene's mission in the Horn of Africa. Each CLI student/pastor had to plant at least one church that planted a church before they could graduate. So CLI became a center for pastoral training and church planting.

John had been teaching for several years when he told me God was directing him to return to his home country to teach his own people and preach the message of holiness.

I was concerned for his welfare because of the continued national conflict and tribal warfare. And he would have to take this treacherous journey on foot. We prayed for John and sent him with our blessing.

For safety, John joined a group of heavily armed traders returning to his country. On this nine-day journey, they crossed rivers swarming with crocodiles and encountered armed bandits. They walked past dead bodies scattered along the paths. They had little to eat, staving off hunger pains by chewing on biscuits. As some slept, others stood guard around their campsites. Walking in daylight hours was more dangerous because would-be killers would easily see them, so they traveled at night.

John was grateful to travel with these traders. But on his return trip, he was not so fortunate. He made this treacherous journey back to Ethiopia alone. God was with him, however, as he safely completed a five-week trip to his homeland (two weeks walking and three weeks teaching).

In three weeks John taught three pastoral training classes (forty hours of instruction for each class) to young men preparing for ministry. John also found time to preach the gospel and share the holiness message. His culture had promised that he would carry much respect as the only surviving, last-born child and that many would listen to him.

And so it was.

A great number of people responded to his preaching and teaching. In those three weeks John planted thirteen new churches in his village and the surrounding areas.

"Today, when you go to my village you can find the whole village worshipping Jesus in the Church of the Nazarene, where my mother and brother help spread the mission of our church—making Christ-like disciples," John says.

As a refugee, John eventually received an opportunity for him and his family to receive funds and become residents of Australia.

This would be a dream come true for anyone who had faced the stark realities of war and famine for most of his life. But after prayerfully considering this opportunity, John and his wife decided to remain in their homeland. Since then, John has completed a theology degree at Africa Nazarene University and has become the country coordinator. John trains teachers and coordinates the overall mission of the Church of the Nazarene in his home country.

In order for a movement of God to be sustained, ministers must be trained and equipped. And that training must be focused on the desired outcome—men and women who make disciples that make disciples, developing churches that develop churches. This teach-reteach principle used in the Horn of Africa was just another biblical principle being put into practice in the phenomenon that took place there.

The Apostle Paul wrote to his disciple, Timothy, "The things you have heard me say in the presence of many witnesses entrust to reliable people who will also be qualified to teach others" (2 Timothy 2:2).

Clearly Paul was encouraging a "teach-reteach" model for Timothy and future disciples to follow. The apostle was passing on teachings he had heard either directly from Jesus or from other apostles in the early church.

"The things you heard me say . . . ," Paul declared to Timothy. Paul then became a first-generation teacher.

Paul's disciple, Timothy, represented the second generation, as he entrusted this teaching to reliable men. Then the reliable men would become the third generation proclaimers of the gospel, passing the teaching on to others, "who would also be qualified to teach."

And this teach-reteach system will continue beyond these four generations until everyone has heard the gospel and been given opportunity to follow Jesus.

Experts evaluating church planting movements say to look for four generations of churches planting churches. The same applies for disciples making disciples and teachers producing teachers. A **multigen-erational, systematic transmission of the message is an important factor behind any movement of God.** It was the practice of the early church and it was an important factor behind the movement in the Horn of Africa.

8

Leading by Team and Mentoring on the Move

*Come, follow me . . . and I will send you
out to fish for people* (Mark 1:17).

They came from all directions—out of the diverse regions of Ethiopia, from the grasslands of South Sudan, and from creative access countries surrounding the Horn. Many came by bus; some walked nine days to reach that bus. Others floated on a river. Still others came by plane. They did this three to four times each year, converging on Addis Ababa, the capital city of Ethiopia. They were responding to my invitation to attend a three-day leadership retreat.

We regularly gathered missionaries, district superintendents, educators, and other senior leaders who worked in this fast-growing, dynamic field. When we gathered, we spent three days in prayer, Bible study, vision casting, and strategy discussions.

The leaders completed reading assignments before they arrived at our conference center: *Houses that Change the World* by Wolfgang Simpson, Neil Cole's *Organic Church*, and *Church Planting Movements* by missionary David Garrison.

We spent most of our time, however, studying the Book of Acts. As we analyzed the biblical model of mission as seen in the Acts of the Apostles, we sought God's plan for the Church of the Nazarene in the Horn of Africa.

At first we addressed the issue of vision. What vision was God giving us in this day? As we studied God's working in the early church, we prayerfully considered this fundamental issue. As we ended our meetings we put our thoughts into writing, publishing a rough draft of our vision statement.

Our district superintendents carried our proposed vision statement to their districts, where they would recreate the leadership agenda with their advisory boards and zone leaders. These district leaders then would comment on our proposed vision statement. At the end of their time together, the zone leaders would meet with the local church pastors. The pastors also commented on the proposed vision statement and offered revisions.

Our pastors, in turn, discussed the matter with their congregations. The people of our churches also prayerfully considered the issue and gave their input.

By the time our district superintendents returned to the next leadership retreat three or four months later they were armed with the thoughts of our Nazarenes throughout the structure of the church. We were always pleased to see that the input from our local leaders and church members raised our expectations of what God wanted to do through us in our area of the world. We prayerfully revised our proposed vision statement. Then the district superintendents returned to their districts and the process of review and revision was repeated.

This process continued until the whole church was united in the vision God gave to us. And it was a big vision, but we all believed that God inspired it. Our vision statement was: *To finish the Great Commission in the Horn of Africa in this generation.*

We also developed a mission statement for the Horn: *To facilitate a holiness, church planting movement in every people group in the Horn of Africa.*

Then the question arose: What strategy would we use to carry out this inspired mission?

The whole church considered these questions in the same way we had reached the vision statement, from the grass roots level.

This process took two years, but when we published our finalized vision and mission statements, we did not need to vision-cast any further. Everyone had participated in prayerfully considering God's will for our church. During those same two years we also identified our DNA—what our identity as a church would be. At the end of those two years we knew who we were, what God expected of us, and how we were to accomplish the task before us.

I had wanted to develop a team with a common cause and a shared strategy. Not only did we achieve that goal at the field level, but it became a reality in the districts, zones, and local churches. We were all individuals with different ministry assignments, but we had one heart, working together as a team with a shared vision and mission that we knew was from Jesus, the Head of the Church.

These leadership retreats were crucial to develop the team, but we also needed to complement retreats with strategic mentoring. I spent much time traveling and ministering with our country coordinators and district superintendents. They followed that example by involving themselves in the activities of the zone leaders, the zone leaders with their pastors, and the pastors with their people.

A culture of mentoring and accountability existed at all levels. Everyone knew the plan, and we worked that plan together. And then in every leadership retreat, our district superintendents reported on how many new disciples[1] had been made and how many new churches had been planted in their districts since the previous leadership meeting. Their reports helped us measure our effectiveness in carrying out the mission God had given us. Developing a leadership team that was passionate about our shared vision and mission was one of the factors behind God's work in the Horn of Africa.

This *Leading by Team* and *Mentoring on the Move* model is not new. Jesus demonstrated this during His years of earthly ministry. We see this as He called the twelve disciples to follow Him. And most of Jesus' ministry was done in the presence of His disciples. He even involved them in His ministry, and when He sent them out, He sent them as pairs or teams. His disciples adopted this practice in the following years, and it was passed on to the Church as an important ministry principle.

The Apostle Paul proficiently developed ministry teams. He developed churches across the world in his missionary travels and then wrote letters to these churches, promoting growth and maturity. And when he traveled, other disciples almost always accompanied him. He was constantly on the lookout for disciples who demonstrated leadership potential. He met Timothy in Lystra. Timothy was already a follower of Jesus, but Paul saw something in him that he wanted to develop. Acts 16:3 indicated that Paul wanted to take Timothy along on the journey. Timothy joined Paul's other traveling companions and they continued their missionary journey throughout Phrygia and Galatia. Timothy became one of Paul's closest allies in ministry.

The Apostle Paul was committed to developing leaders as he traveled in mission. Paul was following the clear example Jesus gave. We were pursuing this same example in the Horn. ***Leading by team* that *mentored on the move*** was another crucial factor behind the movement in the Horn of Africa.

9
Missional Fellowship

They devoted themselves to the apostles' teaching and to fellowship, to the breaking of bread and to prayer. Everyone was filled with awe at the many wonders and signs performed by the apostles. All the believers were together and had everything in common. They sold property and possessions to give to anyone who had need. Every day they continued to meet together in the temple courts. They broke bread in their homes and ate together with glad and sincere hearts, praising God and enjoying the favor of all the people. And the Lord added to their number daily those who were being saved (Acts 2:42-47).

Forty-three denominational leaders from the USA were caravanning seven Land Cruisers from Addis Ababa to Awassa with my wife and me. We had spent the night in Awassa and were now on a long journey to a small village southeast of Awassa, into a very rural region of Ethiopia. After a half day of travel we approached a crowd of about five hundred people sitting on a hillside. They were Nazarenes who had gathered for the weekend in a *Mehaber*.[1]

All of our churches were located within a district and zone. That's a normal structure for the Church of the Nazarene anywhere in the world. However, in the Horn of Africa a zone is divided into *Mehabers*. A *Mehaber* would normally not exceed ten churches. These churches were organized so that no church is more than one day's walk from any other church in the *Mehaber*.

One weekend every month our people gathered to worship the Lord in their *Mehaber*. Pastor and people journeyed to an alternating *Mehaber* location each month.

Every pastor in the *Mehaber* took his turn in preaching. The *Mehaber* leader, usually the most experienced pastor in the *Mehaber*, and the zone leader supervised the preaching and other activities to assure doctrinal and character integrity. Sometimes the district superintendent would be present but not often because so many *Mehabers* took place in his district on the same weekend. Nearly one hundred *Mehabers* might occur in Ethiopia during the same month.

Besides preaching and teaching on holiness the *Mehaber* meetings included other critical components.

The people considered fellowship a priority and would share meals on the grounds. Whether the ladies prepared a special group meal or they shared food they'd brought from their homes, these meals were love feasts.

At the *Mehabers*, new believers are baptized. Those present share the Lord's Supper. Compassionate ministry is another priority at the *Mehaber* meetings. During the weekend the pastor of the hosting church identifies needs of his community. For example, a widow might have a leaking roof that a team will go and repair. Another team may clean the village streets.

As needs are identified, the *Mehaber* sends Nazarenes to meet these needs. This leads to new converts and more disciples for Jesus. Churches are planted and God's kingdom is extended.

Many of the miracles that happened in the Horn of Africa occurred during *Mehaber* meetings. The Nazarenes gathering always expected God to work in their midst. And every activity was bathed in prayer.

As I marveled at the missional fellowship in the *Mehabers*, I realized I was seeing a replica of the early church as portrayed in Acts 2:42-47. Once again disciples were devoting themselves to the apostles' teaching. Fellowship of the believers was rich. Prayer permeated their meetings. God was working in miraculous ways. They shared as needs were identified. And the Lord was adding to their number daily.

I had never seen anything in today's Church that so closely followed the New Testament Church pattern. Every component of the missional fellowship experienced by the early church occurred in these *Mehaber* gatherings.

The *Mehaber* provided the glue to keep the movement going. It was significant in the Horn of Africa.

10

A Driving Passion

*I have great sorrow and unceasing anguish in my
heart. For I could wish that I myself were cursed
and cut off from Christ for the sake of my people*
(Romans 9:2-3).

*Greater love has no one than this: to lay down
one's life for one's friends* (John 15:13).

David lives in Kiech Kuon, a small village in
South Sudan. He is a pastor in the Church of the
Nazarene and serves as the district superintendent of
Sudan South East District. He and his leaders have
planted hundreds of new churches. He's best known,
however, for being late to meetings.

A number of years ago we scheduled a holiness
conference in Addis Ababa. We had constructed a
conference center there, and this conference was a
week-long meeting, at which we'd preach and teach
holiness to our leaders.

We encouraged David to leave early for this conference because Kiech Kuon was far away and David would walk most of it. It would take him two days to walk to the Ethiopian border; then another seven days to reach the nearest public transportation; then two to three days by bus into Addis.

David was not there on the first day of the conference, or on the second day. Late on the third day he finally walked into the meetings.

"Where have you been, David?" one leader asked. "You have missed so much."

David explained that during the first two days of his journey he traveled through villages of his own people. He said he had to talk with them as he passed through their villages, and he found people who did not know Jesus.

"How could I hurry to a meeting when these people did not know Jesus? I'm sorry I'm late, but I planted three churches on the way."

David's apology was quickly accepted.

The next conference David was invited to attend was in Nairobi, Kenya. Our missionaries, district superintendents, and educational leaders throughout the continent were invited for a week of leadership development meetings.

David never showed up.

Three months later I saw David in South Sudan and I chastised him for missing very important teaching in Nairobi.

David told me he could not travel south to Kenya until he acquired a Kenyan visa and to obtain that at that time he had to go to Khartoum, which was north of his village. He'd left home very early. However, he traveled through an area where he'd never been before. He did not speak these villagers' language, but he found one man who knew his language and became David's translator.

David was surprised to discover no one there knew Jesus.

"Howie, how could I hurry to get a visa and attend a meeting somewhere else when none of these people knew Jesus? I just had to preach to them."

Many put their faith in Jesus that day. David formed a Nazarene church for these new believers. He planned to continue his journey to Khartoum, but the people of this newly formed Nazarene church did not know our core values. So he stayed for one month.

"Howie, you would be proud of that church," he said with a smile. "They have become very strong, reaching people in their community and planting churches in nearby villages."

I told David that I was not only proud of that church but also proud of him.

The next meeting David was invited to attend was in Malakal, Sudan, just a three-day walk north of his village. I arrived early to make sure everything was in place before the conference and only one of our leaders was present. Guess who it was.

I told David I was surprised that he was early.

"Yes," David commented, "I am early, but I have a story to tell you!"

After his first day of walking, he had been very hungry and tired. He realized he was approaching a village where he had planted a small Nazarene church.

I will go to the pastor's home and ask to stay at his house tonight, David thought.

He found the pastor outside of his house and asked to spend the night with him. The pastor welcomed him.

"But I am ashamed because I have no food to offer you," the pastor exclaimed. He explained that he could not even borrow food from a neighbor because a severe famine had hit their area. "No one in this entire village has anything to eat."

"Don't worry. I'll rest tonight and be on my journey early in the morning," David said.

They went into the pastor's house and closed the door.

Suddenly a commotion occurred outside. They opened the door to see that an antelope had run in from the bush and dropped dead on the pastor's doorstep.

Not only did David and the pastor eat, but they also invited the entire village to feast. These villagers were mostly animistic people. Animists do not recognize that there is a God who is the Creator, so they worship some part of His creation: the river, a rock, or some created thing. A number of witch doctors also lived nearby. They came for the meal, impressed by how the food was delivered.

David arose before sunrise. He wanted to be on his way so he would make this meeting on time. But when he opened the door the entire village seemed to have gathered outside, patiently waiting for David.

The chief and some elders said they knew he was going to a meeting, but pleaded, "When you go back home, come back through our village."

Were they looking for more antelope? No. They said, "David, we want you to teach us more about Jesus. And then we want to be baptized."

This community has been transformed. These villagers have turned from worshipping spirits in the river and have put their faith and trust in Jesus

Christ. And it's because of one person who just can't go past anyone without asking if that person knows his Jesus.

*** *** ***

Guleed[1] grew up on the streets of his country's capital city.[2] He left home when his mother died and his father remarried. Life on the streets was difficult—and dangerous.

To make matters worse in this nation, anyone who even expressed an interest in Christianity was persecuted. Christians were driven from their homes, disinherited from their families, and excommunicated from their clans and tribes. Following Jesus as the Messiah brought extreme hardship—and often, death.

Guleed fled to a neighboring nation that offered religious freedom. You see, someone had shared Jesus with Guleed on the streets, and he had decided to follow Jesus. As he entered the country that would become his new home, he found the Church of the Nazarene. That's when I met Guleed.

Guleed was passionate about reaching others for Jesus, especially his own countrymen. Many refugees from his country who had escaped the violence and chaos of the political upheaval lived in his new homeland.

I referred him to our ministry council that oversaw the mission to his people group. They provided training and encouraged Guleed to reach his people in his adopted country.

This young man became one of our best evangelists. He routinely led people from darkness into light. Guleed was effective not because of the opportunities he had, but because of the deep passion for his people and his desire to see them come to Jesus.

One day Guleed told us God was asking him to return to his native country. Having warned Guleed of the danger he would face, the ministry council placed their hands on him and asked the Lord to go with him.

Soon after his departure we realized we had not trained him to send his ministry reports to us in a safe, secure way since communications in his native country were wrought with risks of exposure. Our mistake could cost his life.

I was relieved when I heard Guleed's voice on the phone. He had called to tell me he was sending a report to me by email.

Here's my chance to caution Guleed on his report, I thought.

But the phone was disconnected. I anxiously waited for the message to arrive.

Guleed's report came: "I am working on five farms and I am especially irrigating three mango trees. I expect fruit very soon."

Right away I knew which one of us was educated and which one of us was not.

When Guleed traveled from place to place, he rode on top of trucks that carried grain. For a small amount of money the driver would let you sit on top of the load, along with others who had also paid for a ride.

One day as he rode atop a load of corn, gunmen stopped the truck. Two men with AK-47s demanded that the driver give them all of his money. The driver said he'd left his money at home.

They turned to the riders perched on those sacks of corn and ordered them to throw down their money.

"We have no money with us," they cried. These two gunmen opened fire. Guleed was not struck, but the man next to him was.

On another occasion Guleed went to a shoe-shine boy. As he waited for the boy to finish shining the shoes of a customer, another man arrived, carrying an AK-47.

He told the boy to shine his shoes. The small boy said, "Yes, sir, you're next."

"Son, you do not understand. I said shine my shoes. That means do it now!"

The boy rushed to finish the present customer and cried out, "Yes, sir. I will be right with you."

Those were the last words that boy ever spoke. The gunman put the assault rifle to the boy's head and pulled the trigger.

After a number of months Guleed returned to his adopted home country to meet with mission leaders. When he finished his intended business, he told the ministry council, "I am ready to go back. Please pray for me and send me back with your blessing."

Leaders review intelligence reports and up-to-date information about violence and political upheavals before deploying evangelists to ministry assignments.

The council told Guleed that even though things had been difficult in his country, there had just been a turn for the worst and they could not send him back.

"It doesn't matter what happens to me. Please send me back," Guleed begged.

They warned him that he would become a martyr if he returned.

"Seven young men there have recently given their hearts to Jesus," Guleed said. "If I don't go back, who will disciple them?"

Still the council members held their ground.

"Please send me back," Guleed begged. "Eight other young men are very, very close to saying 'yes' to Jesus. If I don't go back, where will they spend eternity?"

I've never forgotten those words: *If I don't go, where will they spend eternity?*

This kind of passion for the lost results in God's transformations. Although Guleed's home country is closed to the gospel, our church is expanding quickly there through the multiplication of disciples and underground churches. Much of what is happening in this country is due to Guleed, and others like him, and their passion for the lost.

❊ ❊ ❊

I was standing in a river in Southeastern Ethiopia. Ten people were on the bank—five men and five women. One at a time they entered the river to be baptized, but before we baptized them, they told us how Jesus had changed their lives.

What powerful testimonies! They told how they knew their sins were forgiven. They told of the joy that had come into their lives. They spoke of the peace that had settled upon them, and they talked about how they no longer felt fear.

And they spoke about the tree.

Right behind me was a mountain. At the top of that mountain was a small village named Hara. The animistic people in that region of Ethiopia believed that Hara was a holy village because it held the biggest tree in the area. The larger the tree in the Horn of Africa, the more likely it would be worshipped.

People didn't know how long ago the tree was planted. They knew it was too large for their fathers to have planted. Not even their grandfathers could have planted it.

How many generations ago did a family member plant that tree? they wondered. So they connected that tree with the spirits of their dead ancestors. And they were terrified of these spirits. They didn't know how well their dead ancestors had been treated, so they believed their ancestors' spirits entered their homes and caused trouble for their families.

They constantly tried to appease these spirits in various ways, including giving the spirits food offerings from their own scant meals.

The ladies who were baptized that day told of a bamboo hut near the tree. Animistic women would walk for days to reach this bamboo hut and wait for men from the village to arrive. Since the village was considered holy, they thought the men who lived there were holy. The husbands of these animistic women sent their wives to Hara to sleep with these holy men, believing that this would bring a blessing to their families.

This is the kind of darkness these people lived in. But these ten people no longer feared the spirits of their dead ancestors—they praised God that they no longer had to seek blessing through such a dark and destructive activity because the Holy Spirit lived in them.

Bekele was the zone leader for that area. He had planted that first Nazarene church—the first church of any Christian denomination—in Hara. As these new believers shared their testimonies, Bekele asked if I would like to see that tree.

"Yes," I exclaimed. "We could take a video of these new Christians' stories right in front of the tree. That will help others see just how much fear these people live with and how God delivered these people out of that fear."

We finished the baptismal service and ate lunch. Then seven of us got into my little white Toyota pick-up. The journey up that mountain took several hours. I still remember driving through the quiet village of Hara and seeing the tree. A tall wall encircled the tree, the bamboo hut, and a large area of land. We opened the gate in the wall and Ermias (our Ethiopian country coordinator at the time), Terry (another American missionary), and I entered the area while the other four lingered outside.

The tree was across the compound. When we reached it, Terry was setting up the camera when I noticed that the others still had not entered the compound. I heard a commotion.

I later found out that a dozen machete-laden "holy" men from that village had approached our leaders and said, "These Americans have desecrated our worship center and are going to die."

"These Americans are not at fault," one of our leaders cried. "We brought them here. If anyone is at fault, we are. Whatever you plan to do to them, do to us instead."

These are the kind of leaders the Church of the Nazarene has in the Horn of Africa, men and women who are willing to die not only for God but also for their missionaries.

The angry villagers pushed our leaders aside and entered the compound, locking the gate behind them.

I turned and saw the men coming toward us with machetes in the air and fire in their eyes. I knew I had only a few moments to live.

Then I saw Worku, a district superintendent from a distant district, fly over the gate. He landed on his two feet and ran to catch these would-be killers, pleading, "Please don't do this!"

These men ignored Worku.

Worku reached into his pocket and pulled out an iPod we had given him a few months earlier.

"This is not a simple cell phone! The Federal Police of Ethiopia gave it to us. They have put us in charge of these Americans' security. I am calling the Federal Police, and they are coming by helicopter!"

He looked up and around, as if to search for approaching helicopters.

These men had never seen an iPod. As they gawked into the sky looking for the helicopters, we walked through the crowd. They never saw us open the gate and run out. My white Toyota pickup had never looked so good. I scurried behind the wheel, raring to go.

But I couldn't leave. Worku was still in the compound with the three leaders.

"Howie, this is critical. Go!" Ermias cried.

"We can't! Our men are still inside!"

"Howie, they will take care of themselves. Goooo!"

The truck fishtailed away. Ermias rolled down the window and called to our leaders to meet us down the mountain.

About an hour later we arrived at the meeting place and found our four leaders waiting. They had freed themselves and had taken a shortcut to our rendezvous.

"Pray for me," Bekele said as we talked. "I'm going back there tomorrow."

"Do you think that's wise?" I asked.

"Howie, how many people did you baptize this morning?"

"Ten."

"Only ten in that village know Jesus. The rest are lost and on their way to hell." He said they had a strategy to reach that village for Christ and had planned a holiness conference for the coming weekend—but if he did not go back and rebuild the relationships with these people, they would not be able to hold this conference.

Then Worku spoke up. "Pray for me too. I am going back to that village. Those people don't know how much Jesus loves them."

I wondered if there was any sacrifice these men would not make to reach the lost. The Apostle Paul urged Christians to offer their bodies as living sacrifices (Romans 12:1). These men were ready to offer their bodies as living sacrifices or even as dead sacrifices, if need be!

✳ ✳ ✳

I've spoken of many factors behind God's movement in the Horn of Africa, but I believe this passion for God and the lost is the main reason God moved in that area of the world in such extraordinary ways. We need to roll up our sleeves and get our hands dirty and work in the trenches of ministry. We need to lay prostrate before God, seeking Him with our whole hearts. We need to see God once again stretch out His hand to heal and perform miracles. We need Him to cleanse our hearts and lead us into holy living. We need to embark on making disciples that make disciples and churches that plant churches. We need to develop a culture of training, teamwork, and mentoring. We must move beyond self-centered fellowship and do mission together.

All of these things are essential for us to experience a movement of God. But nothing trumps passion. Without a driving passion to know God and to lead others into that experience, we will find ourselves still praying for revival to come.

The great passion of men and women such as David, Guleed, Bekele, Worku, and others was behind the transformation of God in the Horn of Africa.

The Apostle Paul expressed this same kind of passion as he wrote to the church in Rome about his anguish that his people, Israel, had been cut off from the Lord. Incredibly, he stated that he would be willing to be "cursed and cut off from Christ for the sake of my people" (Romans 9:3).

Jesus first demonstrated this passion for the lost when He surrendered all of His rights and privileges of God and became man, so He could die for all people. He gave his life so we could live.

Jesus died on the cross for our sins. And the Apostle Paul gave testimony that he had been "crucified with Christ" (Galatians 2:20). The crucifixion he meant was a death to everything that was important to him, except for his life with Jesus.

Of all of the biblical principles put into practice in the Horn of Africa, the most significant was this: Behind the movement in the Horn of Africa was a great passion for God and for all those for whom Jesus died.

About the Author
Dr. Howie Shute

Howie Shute served as a global missionary in the Church of the Nazarene for fifteen years, serving as field director and field strategy coordinator for the Horn of Africa and as assistant to the regional director, responsible for church multiplication and development throughout the African continent. Under his leadership, God has worked in a number of gospel-resistant African countries. Before Howie's call to Africa, he was a manufacturing executive and a pastor.

In 1989, Howie graduated from Nazarene Theological Seminary with a master of divinity degree. In April 2012 Howie was honored with the doctor of divinity degree by Africa Nazarene University in Nairobi, Kenya.

Howie currently serves as the senior pastor at Victory Hills Church of the Nazarene in the Kansas City District.

Notes

Chapter 1

1. Countries were classified as "Creative Access" if their governments consider Christianity to be illegal. The Church must then find creative ways to work in those countries.

2. The 2007/2008 statistical record indicated 122,885 people attending our churches. The statistics in South Sudan, however, had not been updated for four years due to the volatile conditions in that country. The district journals for South Sudan indicated that 24,274 people attended our weekly worship services, when our leaders at that time estimated 100,000. In reality we had approximately 100,000 people in Ethiopia and 100,000 in South Sudan worshipping in Nazarene churches when we departed the Horn of Africa in December 2008. Additionally, fewer numbers attended our churches in our creative access countries.

Chapter 2

1. Akobo, Ethiopia was just across the river from Sudan, at the farthest western point of Ethiopia, not far from Akobo, Sudan.

Chapter 4

1. Names changed for security reasons.

Chapter 5

1. Bona is a major town in southeastern Ethiopia.
2. Mark 8:33-34.
3. Mark 14:66-72.

4. The experience of Spirit baptism is recorded in Acts 2:1-3. Then in verse 4 we find the believers in the streets boldly proclaiming the gospel. They were in the streets because multitudes had gathered for a religious celebration at the temple and these Galileans spoke of God in their own languages. See also verses 6, 8, and 11.

5. See Acts 8:4-17 and 19:1-20. These are just two accounts where the disciples confronted new believers with their need for Spirit baptism.

Chapter 6

1. All of our churches did not succeed in meeting this goal, but many of them did.

2. The experience of heart cleansing that comes through the baptism of the Holy Spirit.

3. Bonsa-Bona District in Southeastern Ethiopia.

Chapter 8

1. For lack of a better measurement tool we considered those who joined our denomination as new disciples. If they became a church member, we expected that they would live up to their membership vow of making disciples that make disciples.

Chapter 9

1. The Amharic word *Mehaber* has two meanings: (1) association or (2) fellowship. Many community and religious organizations use this word to describe their periodic gatherings. Evangelical Christians in Ethiopia use it to describe the *fellowship* their church enjoys when they gather. The Church of the Nazarene has adopted the word to express an extended meeting of *missional fellowship*. When Nazarenes gather for fellowship, mission would be at the center. The Mehaber became an integral part of God's work in Ethiopia and elsewhere across the Horn of Africa.

Chapter 10

1. Name changed.

2. Country and city locations not identified for security purposes.